COMPARING
ANIMAL TRAITS

KOMODO DRAGONS

DEADLY HUNTING REPTILES

REBECCA E. HIRSCH

Lerner Publications ◆ Minneapolis

Lerner Publications Company
A division of Lerner Publishing Group, Inc.
241 First Avenue North
Minneapolis, MN 55401 USA

For reading levels and more information, look up this title at www.lernerbooks.com.

Photo Acknowledgments

The images in this book are used with the permission of: © Guenter Guni/Getty Images, p. 1; © Chi'ien Lee/Getty Images, p. 4; © TeeJe/Getty Images, p. 5 (top); © Dirk-Jan Mattaar/Alamy, p. 5 (bottom); © YAY Media AS/Alamy, p. 6; © Joel Zatz/Alamy, p. 7 (bottom); © dbimages/Alamy, p. 7 (top); © Reinhard Dirscherl/Alamy, p. 8; © imageBROKER/Alamy, p. 9 (top left); © blickwinkel/Alamy, pp. 9 (top right), 26; © Mauricio Handler/National Geographic/Getty Images, p. 9 (bottom); © Gary Nafis, pp. 10, 11 (right); © Lelia Valduga/Moment Open/Getty Images, p. 11 (left); © Laura Westlund/Independent Picture Service, p. 12; © WILDLIFE GmbH/Alamy, p. 13 (top); © Ethan Daniels/Alamy, p. 13 (bottom); © Irina Fischer/Alamy, p. 14; Tui De Roy/ Minden Pictures/Newscom, p. 15 (top left); © Chris Mattison/Alamy, p. 15 (top right); © Ariadne Van Zandbergen/Alamy, p. 15 (bottom); © Michael Grant Wildlife/Alamy, p. 16; © kkaplin/Alamy, p. 17 (left); © Auscape/UIG/Getty Images, p. 17 (right); © BAY ISMOYO/AFP/Getty Images, p. 18; © Richard Susanto/Moment Open/Getty Images, p. 19 (top); © Fletcher & Baylis/Science Source, pp. 19 (bottom), 23 (bottom); © Anthony Bannister/Gallo Images/Getty Images, p. 20; © Ross/Tom Stack Assoc/Alamy, p. 21 (top); © Danita Delimont/Alamy, p. 21 (bottom); © George Grall/National Geographic/Getty Images, p. 22; © Michelle Gilders/Alamy, p. 23 (right); © Wolfgang Polzer/Alamy, p. 24; © Nature Picture Library/Alamy, p. 25 (top); © CTK/Alamy, p. 25 (bottom); Phil Noble/Reuters/Newscom, p. 27 (top left); © Steve Cooper/Science Source/Getty Images, p. 27 (top right); © Miles Barton/naturepl.com, p. 28.

Front cover: © Anna Kucherova/iStock/Thinkstock.
Back cover: © iStockphoto.com/Herianus

Main body text set in Calvert MT Std 12/18. Typeface provided by Monotype Typography.

Library of Congress Cataloging-in-Publication Data

Hirsch, Rebecca E., author.
    Komodo dragons : deadly hunting reptiles / Rebecca E. Hirsch.
       pages cm. — (Comparing animal traits)
    Audience: Ages 7–10.
    Audience: K to grade 3.
    Includes bibliographical references.
    ISBN 978-1-4677-7977-7 (lb : alk. paper) — ISBN 978-1-4677-8268-5 (pb : alk. paper) —
  ISBN 978-1-4677-8269-2 (EB pdf)
    Komodo dragon—Juvenile literature. 2. Komodo dragon—Behavior—Juvenile literature. 3. Komodo dragon—Life cycles—Juvenile literature.
    I. Title.
    QL666.L29H57 2015
    597.95'968—dc23   2014036939

Manufactured in the United States of America
1 — BP — 7/15/15

TABLE OF CONTENTS 4

Introduction
MEET THE KOMODO DRAGON 6

Chapter 1
WHAT DO KOMODO DRAGONS LOOK LIKE? 6

Chapter 2
WHERE DO KOMODO DRAGONS LIVE? 12

Chapter 3
THE DEADLY HUNT OF KOMODO DRAGONS 18

Chapter 4
THE LIFE CYCLE OF KOMODO DRAGONS 24

Komodo Dragon Trait Chart   30
Glossary   31
Selected Bibliography   32
Further Information   32
Index   32

MEET THE KOMODO DRAGON

A Komodo dragon flicks its forked tongue. It is following a scent through the grass. Komodo dragons are reptiles, a kind of animal. Other kinds of animals include insects, fish, amphibians, birds, and mammals.

A Komodo dragon uses its tongue to follow a scent.

All reptiles have certain traits in common. Reptiles are vertebrates, animals with backbones. They are cold-blooded, so they depend on the temperature of the air or water around them to warm or cool their bodies. They have dry skin covered with scales. Komodo dragons share these traits with other reptiles. But some traits set Komodo dragons apart.

A cold-blooded Komodo dragon suns itself to keep warm.

CHAPTER 1

WHAT DO KOMODO DRAGONS LOOK LIKE?

The Komodo dragon is the heaviest lizard in the world. It can weigh up to 366 pounds (166 kilograms). It may grow longer than 10 feet (3 meters). Males are usually larger than females.

Adult female Komodo dragons are usually about 7.5 feet (2.3 m) long and weigh around 150 pounds (68 kg).

Komodo dragons have grayish-brown skin, huge tails, and sharp claws. The skin's dull color helps **camouflage** them against rocky terrain and tall grasses. Tough scales strengthen their rough skin. These scales protect Komodo dragons from scratches

Komodo dragons use their claws for hunting.

and bites. Komodo dragons' strong tails are good for knocking down **prey**. Their sharp claws grab and tear flesh.

A Komodo dragon has a long, forked tongue and short, sharp teeth. Glands loaded with **venom** are hidden in the lower jaw. They give the dragon a venomous bite. The dragon uses the venom to kill prey.

DID YOU KNOW?
A Komodo dragon's **TEETH** are hard to see because they are almost completely covered by the dragon's gums.

KOMODO DRAGONS VS. RHINOCEROS IGUANAS

A rhinoceros iguana climbs over rocky ground. It pauses to snack on plants growing among the rocks. Rhinoceros iguanas eat plants and small animals on the Caribbean Islands where they live. Adult rhinoceros iguanas usually weigh between 10 and 22 pounds (4.5 and 10 kg). Komodo dragons and rhinoceros iguanas look alike in many ways. They have hefty bodies, sturdy legs, and long, thick tails.

The rhinoceros iguana gets its name from the three horns on its nose.

A Komodo dragon (*left*) and a rhinoceros iguana (*right*) both have camouflaged bodies that help them blend in with their surroundings.

Komodo dragons and rhinoceros iguanas are both dull in color. Rhinoceros iguanas can be gray, olive green, or black. As with Komodo dragons, the dull color helps the iguanas blend in with their dry, rocky habitat.

Komodo dragons and rhinoceros iguanas have large heads compared to the size of their bodies. Both have big mouths with many sharp teeth. The rhinoceros iguana has three horns on its snout. Raised scales form these horns. They look like the horns of a rhinoceros.

A rhinoceros iguana stretches its large mouth.

KOMODO DRAGONS VS. MEXICAN MOLE LIZARDS

Mexican mole lizards are one of the strangest-looking reptiles in the world. Mole lizards are much smaller than Komodo dragons. An adult Komodo dragon's body is longer than a motorcycle. A full-grown mole lizard is about the length of a drinking straw.

A mole lizard's body is very thin. Its skin is pink and has many rings. A mole lizard looks like an earthworm or a snake. But it is neither. It is a special kind of reptile that lives underground.

A Komodo dragon walks on four legs. But a Mexican mole lizard has only two legs on the outside of its body. As it crawls like a snake, the tiny legs near its head help pull it along. A Mexican mole lizard's toes have claws for digging.

A Mexican mole lizard looks more like an earthworm than a lizard.

COMPARE IT!

KOMODO DRAGON

VS.

MEXICAN MOLE LIZARD

	HEAD AND BODY LENGTH	
7.5 TO 10.3 FEET (2.2 TO 3.1 M)	◄ ►	**6.8 TO 9.5 INCHES** (17 TO 24 CENTIMETERS)

	MAXIMUM WEIGHT	
366 POUNDS (166 KG)	◄ ►	**0.2 OUNCES** (5 GRAMS)

	SKIN	
Grayish-brown with scales	◄ ►	Pink with rings

CHAPTER 2

WHERE DO KOMODO DRAGONS LIVE?

Komodo dragons stalk across the island of Komodo in Indonesia. Komodo dragons live on a few neighboring islands as well. The volcanic islands have grasslands, savannas, forests, mountains, and beaches. Few people live there. The land is rugged, and the climate is hot and dry. Volcanoes sometimes blast ash and smoke into the air.

Komodo dragons are adapted to the harsh environment. During the dry season, from May to October, fresh water is scarce. Komodo dragons don't need to drink during this time. They get enough water from their food.

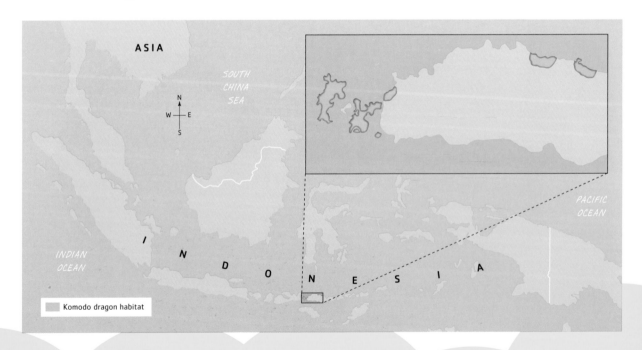

Komodo dragon habitat

DID YOU KNOW?
Komodo dragons are good **SWIMMERS**. They often swim between neighboring islands.

Komodo dragons use their surroundings to warm and cool their bodies. They often live where forests meet grasslands. A dragon moves into the sunny grasses to warm up and retreats into the shady forest to cool off. It uses burrows for sleeping and to keep cool. A dragon may dig a burrow along a dry stream bank or under a boulder or a fallen tree. Some dragons prefer to sleep in dense brush or tall grass.

Komodo dragons are carnivores. They hunt by hiding in bushes or tall grass near animal trails. When prey animals walk by, Komodo dragons pounce. They eat deer, goats, pigs, water buffalo, and even other Komodo dragons. They also scavenge dead animals and snack on small prey such as rodents, birds, and snakes.

A Komodo dragon digs a burrow.

13

KOMODO DRAGONS VS.
AFRICAN SPURRED TORTOISES

An African spurred tortoise crawls out of an underground burrow. It looks around for predators before moving on in search of food. This large turtle lives in Africa along the edge of the Sahara. African spurred tortoises and Komodo dragons live in similar habitats. Both reptiles dwell in places that are hot and dry.

A Komodo dragon (*left*) and an African spurred tortoise (*right*) both live in burrows.

Komodo dragons and African spurred tortoises inhabit grasslands and savannas. Both animals live in burrows. If the tortoise gets too hot, it heads for its cool, sandy burrow. It also smears drool or mud on its front legs to cool itself.

As with Komodo dragons, African spurred tortoises can go weeks without drinking. Both animals get moisture from their food. Komodo dragons get water from meat. African spurred tortoises get moisture from eating leaves and grasses.

DID YOU KNOW?
The African spurred tortoise is one of the largest tortoises in Africa. It weighs about
90 POUNDS (41 kg).

KOMODO DRAGONS VS. YELLOW-BELLIED SEA SNAKES

A yellow-bellied sea snake swims in the ocean. This reptile's habitat is different from the habitat of a Komodo dragon. Komodo dragons live on land. Yellow-bellied sea snakes live in the Pacific Ocean and the Indian Ocean.

Komodo dragons inhabit just a few remote islands. But yellow-bellied sea snakes are widespread. You can find them in the ocean from the coast of eastern Africa to the western coasts of North America and South America. Yellow-bellied sea snakes swim only in saltwater.

A Komodo dragon lives on land but can also swim. A yellow-bellied sea snake lives its entire life at sea. It eats fish and swims with its paddle-shaped tail. It can't survive on land.

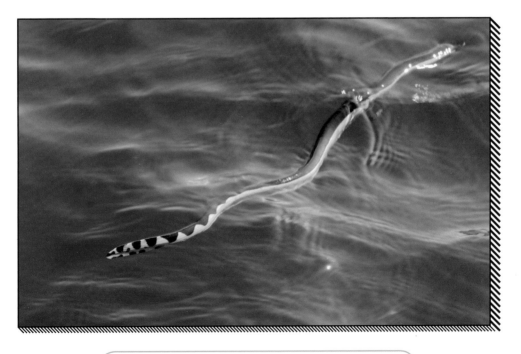

A yellow-bellied sea snake paddles through the water.

COMPARE IT!

KOMODO DRAGON

VS.

YELLOW-BELLIED SEA SNAKE

GRASSLANDS, SAVANNAS, FORESTS, BEACHES, MOUNTAINS	◀ HABITAT ▶	**TROPICAL AND SUBTROPICAL OCEAN WATERS**
ISLAND OF KOMODO AND NEIGHBORING ISLANDS IN INDONESIA	◀ GEOGRAPHIC RANGE ▶	**INDIAN OCEAN AND PACIFIC OCEAN**

Deer, pigs, goats, water buffalo, smaller Komodo dragons

◀ MAIN FOOD ▶

Fish

CHAPTER 3

THE DEADLY HUNT OF KOMODO DRAGONS

A Komodo dragon hides in tall grass near an animal trail.
When a deer walks by, the dragon attacks. It knocks the deer
down with its powerful tail. It bites the animal with sharp teeth
and pulls back with its strong neck. The teeth are serrated, so
they are good for tearing
flesh. The Komodo dragon's
bite opens big, wide
wounds on its prey. Venom
from the dragon's mouth
drips into the wounds.

If the injured deer runs
off, the dragon follows. The
prey animal's wounds are
deep. The venom prevents
blood near the wounds
from clotting (forming
clumps). As the deer loses
blood, the animal weakens
and dies.

Komodo dragons often share food.

The dragon uses its tongue to find the dead animal. It flicks its forked tongue in and out of its mouth. It is sampling scent molecules in the air. With its tongue, it can smell blood from more than 6 miles (10 km) away. Once it finds its prey, the dragon eats. More Komodo dragons may follow the scent and join the feast.

This Komodo dragon caught a deer for dinner.

KOMODO DRAGONS VS. GABOON VIPERS

A Gaboon viper lies perfectly still among fallen leaves. It is waiting for prey to come within striking distance. These large snakes can reach 6 feet (1.8 m) or longer. They inhabit rain forests in central and western Africa. Both Gaboon vipers and Komodo dragons are carnivores, and they hunt in similar ways. Both animals lie still and stay out of sight. A Komodo dragon hides in shrubs or tall grass. A Gaboon viper hides among leaves on the forest floor. As with a Komodo dragon, a Gaboon viper is camouflaged. The viper's patterned skin and leaf-shaped head disappear among the leaves.

A Gaboon viper lies in wait among the leaves.

When a prey animal is near, the viper strikes with lightning speed. The viper's bite, like the bite of a Komodo dragon, contains a deadly venom. The viper holds on to rodents, birds, and frogs until they die from the venom. Larger prey, such as porcupines and antelopes, may escape the snake's grasp. But the venom soon kills the animal. Like a Komodo dragon, a Gaboon viper follows the dying animal's trail. The Gaboon viper smells with its tongue to track down the wounded prey.

A Gaboon viper opens its mouth to strike.

DID YOU KNOW?

Komodo dragons are fast eaters. A 110-pound (50 kg) dragon once ate a 68-pound (31 kg) boar in just SEVENTEEN MINUTES.

KOMODO DRAGONS VS. EASTERN BOX TURTLES

An Eastern box turtle pokes its head out of its shell. These reptiles dwell in woodlands, pastures, and marshes in North America. They inhabit different places than Komodo dragons do. Eastern box turtles behave differently too.

Komodo dragons are carnivores. They sit perfectly still and wait for prey. Box turtles are omnivores. They dine on berries and mushrooms. They also eat animals such as slugs, snails, earthworms, and insects. Box turtles don't hide and wait for prey to come to them. They cross fields and forests and eat whatever they can catch.

Komodo dragons kill their prey with a venomous bite. Box turtles don't have venom. They don't even have teeth! Instead, they use horny ridges on their jaws to catch and chew their food.

An Eastern box turtle searches for food.

COMPARE IT!

KOMODO DRAGON

VS.

EASTERN BOX TURTLE

◄ MAIN FOOD ►

DEER, PIGS, GOATS, WATER BUFFALO, SMALLER KOMODO DRAGONS

SLUGS, SNAILS, INSECTS, AND EARTHWORMS

◄ HUNTING STRATEGY ►

Lie still in tall grass and shrubs

Move through fields and forests

◄ HOW IT CATCHES PREY ►

VENOMOUS BITE

NONVENOMOUS BITE

CHAPTER 4

THE LIFE CYCLE OF KOMODO DRAGONS

Male Komodo dragons wrestle one another during mating season, from May to August. The winners mate with female dragons. About a month later, the female digs a nest in the ground and lays between fifteen and thirty eggs. She lies on the nest and guards the eggs from predators.

Two male Komodo dragons wrestle.

After about nine months in the nest, the eggs hatch. The female leaves the newly hatched Komodo dragons on their own. The hatchlings have green skin speckled with white. Young dragons can't defend themselves from predators—including larger Komodo dragons. Soon after hatching, the young dragons scramble onto trees to avoid predators. Adult dragons are too heavy to climb trees.

A young Komodo dragon perches on a tree.

The young dragons gobble insects, eggs, and geckos. In about four years, the dragons grow too big and heavy to stay in the trees. Then they move to the ground. The dragons keep growing the rest of their lives. As with all animals, they carry traits from their parents. Komodo dragons inherit large, powerful bodies and a taste for meat. With these traits and others, Komodo dragons may survive for thirty years or more.

DID YOU KNOW?
Female Komodo dragons can **REPRODUCE** without mating. Young dragons that are made this way are always male.

KOMODO DRAGONS VS. BURMESE PYTHONS

A Burmese python lies coiled on the ground. This large snake lives in grassy marshes and rain forests of Southeast Asia. Burmese pythons and Komodo dragons have similar life cycles.

Komodo dragons (*left*) and Burmese pythons (*right*) both hatch from eggs.

Like Komodo dragons and many reptiles, female Burmese pythons lay eggs. Burmese pythons usually lay about thirty-five eggs. Just as Komodo dragons guard their eggs, female Burmese pythons also stay with their eggs. The mother coils around the eggs for two to three months until they hatch. From time to time, her body twitches. It looks as if she is hiccuping. This motion creates muscle warmth inside her body, which helps warm the eggs.

After hatching, the young pythons must take care of themselves. Adult Burmese pythons don't eat young pythons, the way adult Komodo dragons eat dragon hatchlings. But the baby pythons do live in trees to avoid predators, just as young Komodo dragons do. When the snakes grow bigger, they move to the ground. Unlike Komodo dragons, adult pythons still sometimes climb trees. Burmese pythons live for about thirty years. This is close to the same life span as Komodo dragons.

KOMODO DRAGONS VS. ARMADILLO LIZARDS

An armadillo lizard scurries across rocky ground. Armadillo lizards live in cracks in rocks in South Africa. Sharp spines cover the reptile's neck, body, and tail. This lizard not only looks different from a Komodo dragon. It has a different life cycle too.

Female armadillo lizards don't lay eggs like Komodo dragons and most reptiles. The lizards give birth to live young. One or two baby lizards are born at a time.

If an armadillo lizard feels threatened, it bites its tail and curls into a spiny ball. This position protects its soft belly and makes the lizard too spiky for predators to eat.

COMPARE IT!

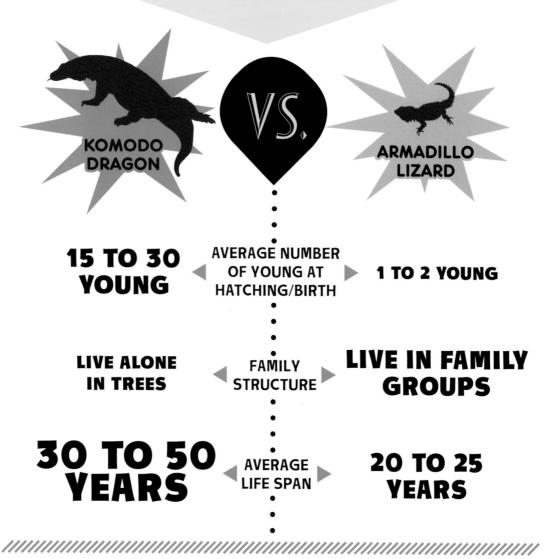

KOMODO DRAGON   VS.   ARMADILLO LIZARD

KOMODO DRAGON		ARMADILLO LIZARD
15 TO 30 YOUNG	AVERAGE NUMBER OF YOUNG AT HATCHING/BIRTH	1 TO 2 YOUNG
LIVE ALONE IN TREES	FAMILY STRUCTURE	LIVE IN FAMILY GROUPS
30 TO 50 YEARS	AVERAGE LIFE SPAN	20 TO 25 YEARS

Komodo dragons live on their own as soon as they hatch. This is not true of armadillo lizards. The young live in groups with adults and other young lizards. As many as sixty lizards may share a rock crevice, although two to six lizards per group is more common. Adults in the family share food with the youngsters. Family living also helps protect the young from predators. Armadillo lizards can live up to twenty-five years, a little less than Komodo dragons.

KOMODO DRAGON TRAIT CHART

This book explores the way gray wolves are similar to and different from other mammals. What mammals would you add to this list?

	COLD-BLOODED	SCALES ON BODY	LAYS EGGS	FORKED TONGUE	VENOMOUS	CARNIVORE
KOMODO DRAGON	X	X	X	X	X	X
RHINOCEROS IGUANA	X	X	X			
MEXICAN MOLE LIZARD	X	X	X	X		X
AFRICAN SPURRED TORTOISE	X	X	X			
YELLOW-BELLIED SEA SNAKE	X	X		X	X	X
GABOON VIPER	X	X		X	X	X
EASTERN BOX TURTLE	X	X	X			
BURMESE PYTHON	X	X	X	X		X
ARMADILLO LIZARD	X	X				X

GLOSSARY

adapted: suited to living in a particular environment

burrows: holes in the ground made by animals for shelter or protection

camouflage: the hiding or disguising of an animal by covering it up or changing the way it looks

carnivores: meat-eating animals

climate: the weather in an area over a long period of time

crevice: a narrow opening caused by a split or crack

geckos: small lizards

habitat: an environment where an animal naturally lives. A habitat is the place where an animal can find food, water, air, shelter, and a place to raise its young.

hatchlings: recently hatched animals

molecules: the smallest particles of a substance

omnivores: animals that eat both plants and meat

predators: animals that hunt, or prey on, other animals

prey: an animal that is hunted and killed by a predator for food

savannas: grasslands containing scattered trees

scavenge: to search for food, such as the remains of prey killed by other animals

serrated: having a jagged edge

traits: features that are inherited from parents. Body size and skin color are examples of inherited traits.

venom: poison produced by some animals and passed to a victim by biting or stinging

LERNER

SOURCE

Expand learning beyond the printed book. Download free, complementary educational resources for this book from our website, www.lernerresource.com.

SELECTED BIBLIOGRAPHY

"Komodo Dragon (*Varanus komodoensis*)." *National Geographic.* Accessed November 6, 2014. http://animals.nationalgeographic.com/animals/reptiles/komodo-dragon/.

"Komodo Dragon, *Varanus komodoensis.*" San Diego Zoo Global. Accessed November 6, 2014. http://library.sandiegozoo.org/factsheets/komodo_dragon/komodo.htm.

O'Shea, Mark, and Tim Halliday. *Reptiles and Amphibians.* New York: Dorling Kindersley, 2001.

"*Varanus komodoensis*: Komodo Dragon." *Animal Diversity Web.* Accessed November 6, 2014. http://animaldiversity.ummz.umich.edu/accounts/Varanus_komodoensis/.

Yong, Ed. "The Myth of the Komodo Dragon's Dirty Mouth." *National Geographic,* June 27, 2013. http://phenomena.nationalgeographic.com/2013/06/27/the-myth-of-the-komodo-dragons-dirty-mouth/.

FURTHER INFORMATION

Crump, Martha L. *Mysteries of the Komodo Dragon: The Biggest, Deadliest Lizard Gives Up Its Secrets.* Honesdale, PA: Boyds Mills Press, 2010. Read about how scientists and explorers are solving the mysteries of the Komodo dragon.

Johnson, Jinny. *Animal Planet™ Atlas of Animals.* Minneapolis: Millbrook Press, 2012. Travel around the world and explore the planet's incredible animal diversity in this richly illustrated book.

Smithsonian National Zoological Park: Komodo Dragon

http://nationalzoo.si.edu/animals/reptilesamphibians/facts/factsheets/komododragon.cfm
Visit this site from the Smithsonian National Zoological Park for information on Komodo dragons.

Wildscreen Arkive: Komodo Dragon (*Varanus komodoensis*)
http://www.arkive.org/komodo-dragon/varanus-komodoensis
This site from the wildlife group Wildscreen Arkive features photos, video, and audio clips of the Komodo dragon and information about its biology and habitat.

INDEX

Komodo dragon comparisons: vs. African spurred tortoises, 14–15; vs. armadillo lizards, 28–29; vs. Burmese pythons, 26–27; vs. Eastern box turtles, 22–23; vs. Gaboon vipers, 20–21; vs. Mexican mole lizards, 10–11; vs. rhinoceros iguanas, 8–9; vs. yellow-bellied sea snakes, 16–17

Komodo dragons: habitat, 12–13, 17; hunting behavior, 13, 18–19, 23; life cycle, 24–25; prey, 18–19, 23, 25; size, 6, 11; traits, 6–7

reptile traits, 5

trait chart, 30

types of habitats: deserts, 14; islands, 8, 12; oceans, 16; rain forests, 20, 26; woodlands, 22